XTREME HORROR LAB

THE SCIENCE OF SEA MONSTERS

A&D Xtreme
BOLD HI-LO NONFICTION
An imprint of Abdo Publishing
abdobooks.com

ANNA ANDERHAGEN

TAKE IT TO THE XTREME!

GET READY FOR AN EXTREME ADVENTURE! THE PAGES OF THIS BOOK WILL TAKE YOU INTO THE SPOOKY WORLD OF UNEXPLAINED PHENOMENA. WHEN YOU HAVE FINISHED READING THIS BOOK, TAKE THE XTREME CHALLENGE ON PAGE 43 ABOUT WHAT YOU'VE LEARNED!

ABDOBOOKS.COM
Published by Abdo Publishing, a division of ABDO, PO Box 398166, Minneapolis, Minnesota 55439.

Printed in the United States of America, North Mankato, MN.
052024
092024

THIS BOOK CONTAINS RECYCLED MATERIALS

Design: Kelly Doudna, Mighty Media, Inc.
Production: Mighty Media, Inc.
Editor: Jessica Rusick
Cover Photograph: DNY3D/Adobe Stock
Interior Photographs: AF Fotografie/Alamy Photo, pp. 16–17; Anatoly Vartanov/Shutterstock Images, pp. 34–35; Andrey Armyagov/Adobe Stock, pp. 12–13; bayazed/Adobe Stock, pp. 40–41; Benedikt von Imhoff/AP Images, pp. 24–25, 30–31; Benny Marty/Adobe Stock, pp. 22–23; DNY3D/Adobe Stock, p. 1; Fer Gregory/Shutterstock Images, p. 42; grandfailure/Adobe Stock, pp. 4–5; history_docu_photo/Alamy Photo, pp. 6–7; Jason Kennedy/Shutterstock Images, pp. 18–19; lev radin/Shutterstock Images, pp. 38–39; Lobo Media/Shutterstock Images, pp. 20–21; MEGAN LOVETT/AP Images, pp. 26–27; N. Steele/Shutterstock Images, pp. 10–11; Olaus Magnus/Wikimedia Commons, pp. 8–9; swillklitch/Adobe Stock, pp. 28–29; Tkachuk Oksana/Adobe Stock, p. 45; valkoinen7/Adobe Stock, p. 44; Victor1153/Shutterstock Images, pp. 32–33; Wikimedia Commons, pp. 14–15; Wm. Leo Smith/Wikimedia Commons, pp. 36–37
Design Elements: Dominik Hladik/Shutterstock Images (moon); nikiteev_konstantin/Shutterstock Images (curves); pixelparticle/Shutterstock Images (stars); pixssa/Shutterstock Images (stretchy circle)

LIBRARY OF CONGRESS CONTROL NUMBER: 2023949420

PUBLISHER'S CATALOGING-IN-PUBLICATION DATA
Names: Anderhagen, Anna, author.
Title: The science of sea monsters / by Anna Anderhagen
Description: Minneapolis, Minnesota : Abdo Publishing, 2025 | Series: Xtreme horror lab | Includes online resources and index.
Identifiers: ISBN 9781098293222 (lib. bdg.) | ISBN 9798384912491 (ebook)
Subjects: LCSH: Sea monsters--Juvenile literature. | Monsters--Juvenile literature. | Giant squids (Monsters)--Juvenile literature. | Sea serpents--Juvenile literature. | Science--Juvenile literature.
Classification: DDC 130--dc23

TABLE OF CONTENTS

CHAPTER 1

SEA BEAST

A large shadow emerges beneath you while you're swimming in the ocean. A beast reveals its scaly head and red eyes. It opens its mouth and shows its sharp teeth! You scream and the beast disappears. Was it your imagination or did you just see a sea monster?

In 1926, author H.P. Lovecraft wrote a story about a monster called Cthulhu (kuh-THOO-loo) that lived under the sea.

CHAPTER 2

MYSTERIOUS DEPTHS

Humans have only explored 5 percent of the ocean. This means many sea creatures remain unknown. Scientists discover thousands of new ocean **species** each year. Who knows what kinds of monsters could be **lurking** underneath the sea?

Ancient Greek mythology includes many stories of sea monsters, such as Scylla (*top*).

ISLANDIA
MARE GLACIALE
FARE
AMBRA SPERMA CETI
ZIPHIUS
PISTR SIVE PHISET
TILE
BALENA
D
ORCAD
HET LANDIA
NORMORIA
NORVEGIA REGNUM
TILEMARCHIA
VALDRES
HELGALA
TRONDO
FROSTEN
MARE DEUCALIDONICUM
SCOCIE PARS
AMPLISSIMUM REGNI SCOTORUM
OCEANUS BRITANICUS
ANGLIE PARS
G
MARE GERMANICUM
DANIA
HOLSATHIA
VERMIS 40 PE LO
SCUTENES
HIS CLIPEIS SIGNA PONES VIRTUTIS SORTA UT PROBITAS GENERIS LUCEAT IPSA TUI
PAULUS PAPA III

Sailors have told stories of sea monsters for thousands of years. They've told tales of the Kraken, sea **serpents**, and the Loch Ness Monster. These sea monsters are all cryptids.

A cryptid is an animal that has not been proven to exist. Many people believe in these cryptids and seek proof that they are real.

Between 1527 and 1539, Swedish clergyman Olaus Magnus created the Carta Marina, a map showing where sailors had encountered mysterious sea monsters. It helped warn sailors about the dangers of the ocean.

CHAPTER 3

THE KRAKEN

Some legends describe the Kraken as 1.5 miles (2.5 km) long with arms as big as ship masts.

The Kraken is said to live in the northern Atlantic Ocean between Norway and Greenland. Long ago, people said the Kraken was so big that it looked like an island. When a ship got too close, the Kraken grabbed it and pulled it underwater.

XTREME FACT

The earliest stories of the Kraken are from the 1100s.

People could tell the Kraken was coming when the water turned brown and a horrible smell filled the air. When the Kraken dove deep into the water, it caused a **whirlpool**. The whirlpool dragged ships and sailors down into the depths of the sea, never to be seen again.

Whirlpools can form naturally in the ocean. The Saltstraumen strait near Norway is known for having strong whirlpools.

CHAPTER 4

SEA SERPENTS

Ancient Greek art often showed the mythological hero Heracles fighting the Hydra.

People in many cultures tell sea **serpent** stories. Hindu **mythology** spoke of sea serpents called Nagas. In Japanese mythology, Yamata no Orochi was a water serpent with eight heads and tails. In Greek mythology, Hydra was a giant sea serpent with many heads. If one head was cut off, two new heads would grow in its place.

In the 1500s, sailors told stories of a sea **serpent** called Soe Orm. It was 200 feet (61 m) long with sharp scales and flaming eyes. Soe Orm swam in the northern Atlantic Ocean near Norway and attacked ships.

Olaus Magnus published a drawing of Soe Orm in 1555.

More than 100 people reported seeing a sea **serpent** in the early 1800s off the shores of Massachusetts. Some people described it as 100 feet (30.5 m) long. It had a head like a horse's. Armed boats found the sea serpent and fired **musket** balls at it. The sea monster swam away.

The Massachusetts sightings were near Cape Ann, a peninsula in northern Massachusetts.

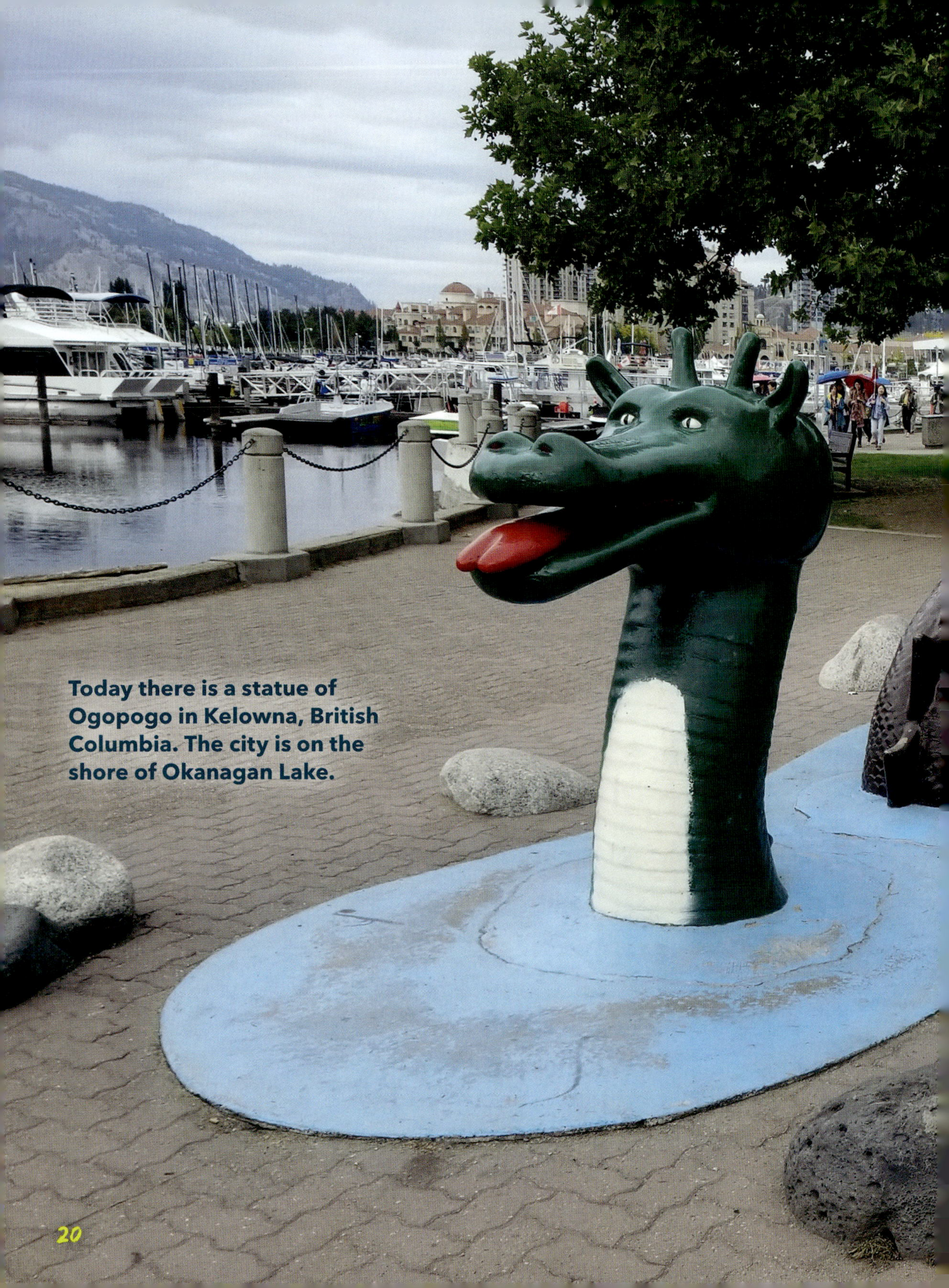

Today there is a statue of Ogopogo in Kelowna, British Columbia. The city is on the shore of Okanagan Lake.

People have told stories of a sea **serpent** named Ogopogo at Okanagan Lake in Canada for generations. Okanagan Lake is 75 miles (120 km) long and 771 feet (235 m) deep. Most people say the serpent is green and black. It has the head of a horse or sheep.

CHAPTER 5

LOCH NESS MONSTER

The town of Drumnadrochit is on the shore of Loch Ness. It has a museum dedicated to the Loch Ness Monster.

One of the best-known sea monsters is the Loch Ness Monster. Most people describe the Loch Ness Monster as having a long neck, fins, and humps. Thousands of people think they have seen the Loch Ness Monster, but no one has proven it is real.

XTREME FACT

Loch Ness is a lake in Scotland. It is 23 miles (37 km) long and 788 feet (240 m) deep. Because it is so deep, Loch Ness has very dark, chilly water.

Another large sonar search was carried out in August 2023. Skipper Ali Matheson was one of the volunteers who participated.

It is hard to see underwater in Loch Ness. **Sonar** allows people to see underwater with sound waves. In 1987, **marine biologist** Adrian Shine led a 20-boat sonar search for the Loch Ness Monster. They found three large underwater objects that could not be explained.

In 2023, French tourist Etienne Camel was taking pictures of Loch Ness. He saw a 65-foot (19.8 m) dark shape moving beneath the surface. He took a picture of the mysterious shape before it disappeared.

Dan Taylor used a submarine to look for the Loch Ness Monster. He died in 2005 without finding proof the monster existed.

CHAPTER 6

WHY DO PEOPLE BELIEVE?

The open ocean can be a scary place. So much beneath the surface is unknown. People use sea monster stories to explain or understand the unknown. With each retelling of the stories, the monsters may change or become **exaggerated**. And every person sees what is in the water differently.

Sailors on the ocean face many real dangers, such as storms with strong winds and huge waves.

There must be concrete evidence of a creature to prove it exists. This can be a skeleton or a body washed onto shore. Scientists have been looking for evidence that sea monsters exist for centuries. They haven't found concrete proof yet.

Willie Cameron and others have taken photos of what they think are sea monsters. But the photos are not clear enough to prove sea monsters are real.

Many descriptions of sea monsters include **characteristics** of existing sea animals. The many arms of the Kraken could be octopus arms. There are sea snakes in the ocean. Water could **distort** their bodies to make them look longer than they actually are.

Giant Pacific octopuses have more than 2,000 suction cups on their arms.

CHAPTER 7
SCIENTIFIC POSSIBILITIES

The Moskvarium Oceanography and Marine Biology Center in Moscow, Russia, has a display featuring a giant squid attacking a whale.

Many scientists believe that people have been mistaking giant squids for the Kraken. Giant squids live in the ocean. They are commonly found near Norway and Greenland. They can be longer than 40 feet (12 m).

XTREME FACT

Giant squids have the largest eyes of any living being. Each eye of a giant squid can be as large as a human head.

A giant oarfish is snake-shaped and can be 50 feet (15 m) long. It has a bright red **dorsal** fin running down its back. Some people have reported seeing a

In 1996, US Navy SEALs found a dead 23-foot (7 m) giant oarfish on the beach in Coronado, California.

sea **serpent** wash up on shore, only to find out later it was a giant oarfish.

In 2023, a plesiosaur skeleton was sold at an auction of items related to natural history.

Dead basking sharks are also mistaken for sea monsters. Many fishermen have caught dead basking sharks and thought they were **prehistoric** plesiosaurs. Basking sharks can be more than 40 feet (12 m) long. The shark's gills rot after death and make it look like it has a long neck.

XTREME FACT

Some people think the Loch Ness Monster could also be a prehistoric plesiosaur. These giant reptiles with four flippers went extinct 66 million years ago.

In 2018, scientists collected water samples from Loch Ness to test the **DNA** of animals living there. Scientists found that thousands of large eels live in Loch Ness. This led some scientists to believe that the Loch Ness Monster could actually be an eel.

XTREME FACT

One Loch Ness Monster hunter believes the monster might be a giant Wels catfish. They can weigh more than 600 pounds (272 kg) and be 9 feet (2.7 m) long.

The European conger is the largest eel species. The eels can be nearly 10 feet (3 m) long.

CHAPTER 8

SCIENCE VS. STORIES

Sea monster stories have **evolved** over hundreds of years. Some scientists think that people mistake real animals for sea monsters. However, scientists agree that thousands of ocean animal **species** remain undiscovered. Do you believe in sea monsters?

XTREME CHALLENGE

TAKE THE QUIZ BELOW AND PUT WHAT YOU'VE LEARNED TO THE TEST!

1) What is a sea monster?

2) Name three kinds of sea monsters.

3) Why do you think people believe in sea monsters?

4) What ocean animals are associated with sea monsters?

5) After reading this book, do you believe in sea monsters?

SEA MONSTER HORROR LAB

Water can make sea creatures appear larger than they are. Try this experiment to see how water changes the way things look.

WHAT YOU NEED

- page from a newspaper or magazine
- sealable clear sandwich bag
- water

WHAT YOU DO

1. Place the newspaper or magazine page on a waterproof workspace.

2. Fill the sandwich bag at least three-fourths full of water. Seal the bag.

3. Place the bag of water on the newspaper or magazine page. Look through the bag at the

images or words on the page. How do they look?

4 Lift the sealed edge of the bag up slightly. What do you notice when looking through the bag at the page? Does anything change?

WHAT HAPPENED?

Light travels at different speeds through different materials. It travels slower through water than air. When light slows down, it bends. Light bends as it passes through the water in the plastic bag. This **distorts** the way things underneath the bag look.

TAKE IT FURTHER

Try wiggling the bag while looking at the newspaper or magazine. Motion will distort the words and images even more. Imagine what waves in the ocean can do to magnify and distort a creature underwater!

GLOSSARY

characteristic–a quality or a feature of something.

distort–to twist something out of its normal shape or condition.

DNA–a material in the body that helps determine what features an organism will inherit. DNA stands for "deoxyribonucleic acid."

dorsal–relating to or located on the top or back.

evolve–to develop gradually.

exaggerate–to make something seem larger or greater than it actually is.

lurk–to wait in a somewhat hidden place.

marine biologist–a scientist who studies ocean life.

musket–a long gun used from the 1600s to the 1800s that shot round, lead balls.

mythology–a collection of myths from a certain group of people.

prehistoric–existing in time before people began to write.

serpent—a snake.

sonar—a device that uses sound waves to detect the presence and location of objects underwater.

species—a group of related living beings.

whirlpool—an area where water moves quickly in a circle and draws floating objects toward its center.

ONLINE RESOURCES

Booklinks
NONFICTION NETWORK
FREE! ONLINE NONFICTION RESOURCES

To learn more about sea monsters, please visit **abdobooklinks.com** or scan this QR code. These links are routinely monitored and updated to provide the most current information available.

INDEX